Horse Training

Arabian Horse Elegance: A Thorough Manual On The Proper Care, Training, And Collaboration With These Magnificent Equines, Discover The Splendour Of Arabian Horse Care: Professional Advice For Achieving Success And Balance

BurkhardRiemer

TABLE OF CONTENT

The Paddock And Stall For Horses................................... 1

Taking A Bath 17

Suggestions For Natural Height Raising......................31

Ways To Improve Your Classes On Horse Riding...67

A Variety Of Appropriate Balancing And Fundamental Suppling Exercises 86

After The Ride: Valuable Teachings On Horsemanship 132

The Paddock And Stall For Horses

If you can house your Arab in a horse stall with a paddock, that would be ideal. In technical terms, it should really be named a horse shelter rather than a horse stall. To keep the horse in for at least the night, a stall should measure at least 12 by 12 feet and be closed on all four walls with a closed door. A horse shelter is open and closed on three sides, allowing the horse to enter and exit whenever it pleases.

There might be an access door in the shelter where you can feed your Arab twice a day and bring them in or out. My shelters feature a split-half door that we may leave ajar so that your Arab can frequently peek out. Feeding access is also provided from the top opening. When bad weather is predicted for the night, we shut the top door.

The grain feeder is fixed to the inside of the shelter's bottom entrance, and I can access the hay rack to the right of the door. In this manner, I can add a few hay flakes to the rack and fill his feeder with a tiny pail of grain without having to open the bottom door. To lessen the amount of hay that he spills on the ground, one Arab needs a hay bag. For convenient feeding, the front glass also provides access to the bag.

The shelters are 12 by 12 feet. The paddocks ought to measure a minimum of 25 by 50 feet or more. You might need to do some research to find your Arab the ideal living space if you don't own a horse property and are boarding him at a facility or tiny stables. A daily turnout stall is not something we advise unless your objective is an Arabian Show horse.

We advise having a pasture shelter for your Arab horse if you choose to keep him as a full-time pasture horse. Should your Arab be kept on your land, you will need to remove the dung from the paddocks regularly. You can want to employ someone to fix small things around your property and tidy the paddocks. It is recommended that you clean the paddocks yourself either every day or every other day. The rationale behind this is that the more times you do it, the less effort it requires and the fewer insects and parasites your horse will have to deal with.

After seven days in the cold, I cleaned paddocks. Every paddock held an ample amount of manure. You have a lot of work ahead of you if the weather prevents you from cleaning. Because of this, we advise daily cleaning whenever it is practical. Until the manure transforms into fertilizer, it should be kept in a manure bin. You have two options: either scatter the fertilizer over your pastures or charge $10 per truckload for it. Gardens can also take advantage of it. You can either purchase or hire a tractor with a front-end loader and mower if you own a horse stable. When the weeds start to grow, you can use the tractor to mow your pastures at least twice a year. Once a month, you can mix your manure mound with the front-end loader.

Twice a year, you can spread fertilizer using a front-end loader. A harrow might also be used to aid in spreading the manure over the pasture. Here are a few benefits of boarding at a local stable for your horse. You just pay your board dues each month. The owner of the stable is in charge of all general farm care, including purchasing a tractor and implements, cleaning manure, and providing feed.

Additionally, the contract states that the owner shall provide you prompt notice if any health issues emerge. In case of an emergency, you should also provide the stable owner with your veterinarian's phone number. It is actually a pretty good deal if you just have one Arab, and the cost is between $400 and $500 in your location. Plus, you get to spend more time with your new best buddy face-to-face!

Why a pasture and Stall for horses are ideal

For Arabs, a horse stall and pasture usually work best. Your Arab will be able to move freely within or outside a paddock and horse stall. Despite spending the night locked in the paddock every night, he feels more liberated. When you bring your Arab inside and when you let him out, it will be entirely up to you. The grass will grow at its fastest in the late spring and early summer.

As was previously noted, an Arab may become unsteady due to excessive grass sugar concentration. Your Arab could die from laminitis caused by the founder. Euthanizing an afflicted horse is a very unpleasant procedure that occurs frequently.

We only let our horses go outside for two to three hours a day during the season of rapid growth. We receive a lot of rain in the autumn, winter, and spring. The pasture is unsuitable for horses, and the rain creates pools. We only let them graze for one or two hours each day, and on certain days, we don't let them out at all.

On most other days, if the weather permits, we might let them outside for up to ten hours a day. I attempt to let them outside whenever I can because they graze for exercise for the entire time and consume roughly one pound of grass every hour. I just need to feed the horses roughly 10 pounds of hay per night if they are out for 10 hours. Thus, all parties benefit.

Your Arab always wants to graze and exercise over hay, and they always prefer fresh pasture grass. When grazing all day, your Arab will cover about 8 miles of walking each day. Additionally, your hay expenses are reduced. Every year, your Arab will consume 7300 pounds of hay or grass. For a single horse, 65 bales of hay would be needed if you were to purchase 3-string bales at a cost of 110 pounds apiece and feed your horse exclusively hay—not pasture grass. Each year, you can get a whole semi-trailer load of hay for a reasonable price per bale. Alternatively, you can purchase 10–20 bales at a time individually.

Here in my area, we spend close to $23.00 per bale for 3-string orchard grass. For each horse, the cost of hay alone would exceed $100.00 per month at such price. Each horse needs thirty pounds of vitamins per month. Each 50-pound bag of vitamins costs $23.00 and is sufficient to serve one horse for 50 days. The COB costs $12.00 for fifty pounds, which is significantly less. A horse can use one bag of COB for approximately one month.

Horse treats come in 20-pound sacks, costing $12.00 each, and one bag will sustain a horse for almost three months. As you can see, when your horse spends less time in the pasture, the costs increase. Here are some additional benefits of boarding your equine. You and your Arab would, however, prefer a paddock with a shelter and daily pasture time, whether you board or own a horse property.

Give your Arabian a few days to adjust to the Stall. Your new home will seem foreign to your Arab when you bring him here. Having a pasture buddy makes the majority of Arabs the happiest. Your horse will have a partner to share the pasture with at turnout time if there is another horse in the connecting paddock. The stalls are frequently connected yet distinct. Since they can frequently hear each other breathe, snort or whine in the attached Stall, neither horse will feel lonely during the night.

When your Arab has spent two to three days getting acquainted with his pasture buddy and paddock, it's a good idea to start developing a relationship with your horse. Just put on his halter and give him a good brushing on the first day. After giving him a brief tour, put him back in his paddock. You can do the same on the second day, but this time, saddle him up, put on his harness, and take him for a short stroll. Increase your activities with him little by little each day that you work with him. After a week or so of warm-up exercises, do not attempt to ride him.

Choosing the Ideal Home for Your Arabian

Although we have discussed a lot of this already, your horse must have the proper housing and surroundings. We've discussed the benefits of having your horse in a paddock with a shelter and a pasture buddy to keep him company when he spends nearly all of his time in the pasture.

You will have far greater control over your Arab's welfare if you own the land where your horses are kept. It's not exactly perfect, but you might have to choose the greatest place if you're boarding your Arab. There might not be a lot of options available to you. There might only be two or three stables in the neighbourhood. For a variety of reasons, you might take your Arab to one place and then shift him to your second choice a month later. You need to think about the needs for care, nutrition, a pasture buddy, communication with the stable owner, and shelter.

If your Arab gelding is an "Alpha" and his pasture buddy is an Alpha as well, you may have to move him since the two horses are fighting. You must get along well with the stable owner if you are boarded. Do not be afraid to advise him to find another horse with whom your Arab will get along. You won't have to relocate your Arab ever again if a better pasture buddy can be found. An Arabian horse that is young may experience trauma if it is moved too frequently.

Where to Get on Your Arabian

The only choice available to you if you don't own a horse property is to board your Arab. It is not unusual for a horse owner to purchase a second horse and then a third. Financial issues become important very early if you are boarding. You might start thinking about buying a small stable for you and your horses to live in instead of boarding if your monthly rent or house payment is $1200.00 and your monthly boarding expenses are between $1000.00 and $1500.00. If your study indicates that a 3-bedroom house and a 5-acre horse ranch would cost about $1900.00 for a mortgage, you might decide that this is less expensive than boarding. Even some maintenance expenses and food would be covered by your ample funds. Please remember to account for the entire amount of time needed for maintenance.

Your time for regular ranch maintenance will be much reduced if you work 40 hours a week and can only spend 20 hours with your horses. Often, the extra time will take up time that you could have spent with your horses.

Taking A Bath

You might feel the need to give your new best friend lots of baths. But remember, his skin and hair are kept healthy by his natural oils. Washing too much can remove those oils. It is, therefore, preferable to wash your Arab just once a season, during the warm months. Ensure that you purchase a warm-water washing stall and high-quality horse shampoo, such as Mane & Tail Shampoo.

Take your Arab with you into the laundry room.

2. Attach your Arab's Lead Rope to the hitching rail with care now.

3. You can turn on the water once your Arab is inside the washing machine.

Use your fingertips to feel the water's temperature before soaking your Arab. Make sure the water is lukewarm and pleasant.

4. After thoroughly wetting your Arab's body, start massaging in the shampoo to produce a little foam. Take care not to use so little that you can't get a rich lather or so much that you can't rinse it all out. Do your best to stay out of his mouth and eyes. Rinse face when bathing if needed.

5. Tip: Give his head the last wash. This is the bit he would find objectionable.

6. Now, give him a good rinse with warm water.

Using your hands, gently massage the shampoo from top to bottom. Repeat this a few times to remove all of the shampoo so that his natural oils can start working to keep him healthy.

7. Now shut off the water and use a towel to pat him dry. Give him a good massage. Take him to a place where he can dry off in the sun. Remember that as soon as he gets the chance, right after getting bathed, he will roll in the mud or dirt. It is best to wait until he is totally dry before allowing that to occur.

paws

When running and walking, your Arab needs to be able to grip with his hooves. Each time you remove your Arab from the stall, you should clean his hooves. You would be familiar with how to remove dirt, manure, and other debris from the hooves with a hoof pick. It is crucial because tiny gravel fragments might become lodged and hurt your Arab. Cleanse each hoof by picking up each foot separately.

The majority of horses require hoof trims every six to eight weeks. You may either hire a farrier to come and trim for you, or you can learn how to do this with a trimmer and file. The trimmer resembles a hybrid of a nail clipper and a set of enormous pliers. The rough file is really huge. Most of the time, the hoof can be filed smoothly in a few strokes after reducing it to a ¼ to ½ inch. Avoid cutting the hoof too short, as this may cause bleeding. After clipping, some horse owners choose to always shoe their mount.

Some horses can walk anywhere without shoes because of their extremely strong hooves. Some people find it difficult to walk on jagged pebbles or stones. Strap-on shoes are an additional choice. These can be taken off when not needed and put on when needed. You may choose to wear shoes exclusively on your front two feet. Since Arabs place the majority of their weight on their front foot, this is frequently sufficient.

At the very least, you should have a farrier trim your horse when you initially get it done. Should you want to trim yourself in the future, please take great care with the trimming. Costly are farriers. "You need to start with a large fortune if you want to have a small fortune after owning horses for a few years," it is said. Another proverb goes, "The human brain is the most amazing organ in the human body; it thinks and functions well every day, 365 days a year, from the moment of your birth, until you fall in love with a horse." Thus, you might use this as a caution about the total cost of owning your horse in the long run.

As you read this book, we anticipate that it will already be too late for you. Either you already have feelings for your horse, or you already have feelings for the concept of purchasing your first Arab. In any case, it's probably too late to heed any caution. I have also underlined the potential for risk with Arabs. It is estimated that 100 deaths annually in the United States are related to riding or handling horses; most of these deaths are accidental, and the Arabs did not intend to kill the victim. An estimated 1000–2000 head injuries occur annually, most of which are treated with survival but leave the victim permanently altered. Again, for this reason, we advise you to use a safety helmet when riding.

The Teeth of Your Arab

Horses have teeth designed for grazing.

There are 12 incisors in the front of the mouth of an adult horse.

The premolars and molars are two of the 24 teeth that are designed for chewing.

"Tushes" are the extra four canine teeth that stallions and geldings have located just beneath their incisors.

In front of the molars, some horses—male and female alike—will also acquire one to four tiny vestigial teeth, or "wolf," teeth.

A horse's teeth can be used to determine how old it is.

Throughout life, teeth erupt and become worn down from grazing.

Horses experience variations in the angle at which the chewing surfaces touch, as well as a characteristic wear pattern and tooth form.

Horses' ability to digest food is hampered if their teeth lack a flat surface on which to chew.

Regular dental examinations are a good idea, but no more than once a year is recommended.

Typically, veterinarians advise having your Arab dog's teeth floated every one to four years, but ideally by the time the animal is ten years old.

The act of filing down all of the sharp points and edges to create a level chewing surface is known as "floating" your horse's teeth.

Increased revenue and outlays for your budget!

Eyes: Of all land mammals, horses have the largest eyes.

Horses can see over 350 degrees, and they have great day and night vision.

Similar to red-green colour blindness in humans, horses have partial colour blindness.

Your veterinarian should examine your Arab's eyes on a regular basis. Every day, you ought to examine your Arab's eyes. Regular inspection of his stall and paddock is necessary to remove any sharp or pointed objects, such as loose nails or screw tips poking through.

Additionally, search for and remove any loose, sharp wires or splinters. The rationale is that your Arab runs the risk of getting an eye-piercing. During one of your routine observations, you might see that your Arab's eye is almost completely swollen shut. It's likely that your Arab just has a small piece of grass, dust, or dirt in his eye. Try using a medicine called "Vetericyn" Ophthalmic Gel for irritated eyes before calling the veterinarian. After cleaning your hands, apply a thick layer of gel to your fingertip and place it slightly above his lower eyelid. He'll undoubtedly want to move away from you but resist the urge to let him touch your hand with his eye. His eye is itching, and it feels wonderful, so he'll want to do that. This will assist in distributing the gel across his eyeball's surface.

Should the oedema not subside within a day, you can choose to schedule a stable appointment with your veterinarian. Even after losing one eye to blindness, some horses can still be ridden and function normally most of the time. Some horses go totally blind, but if there's no possibility of a stumble, they could be able to be ridden in mild terrain. That would only happen in a lifetime partnership between a really strong horse and rider. This book is actually meant to educate you on how to create, tend to, and grow that same kind of lifetime relationship.

The lifespan of a horse is 25 to 30 years. There are Arabs who survive into their 40s and sometimes even older. In the 1800s, there was a horse that was reported to have lived for 62 years. A 56-year-old pony is said to have passed away in 2007. The relationship and affection you share with your Arab will only deepen with each passing year, even though the majority of it will blossom in the first year. I like to put my chest against my Arab's neck, rub my face against his, and hug him around the base of his neck. I used to do this with him before I bought him to make sure he was a loving Arab that I could get to know.

Suggestions For Natural Height Raising

People frequently believe incorrectly that you only need to control your intellect in order to control your heart. This is the reason why teaching a horse how to halt and start requires the use of a lead line or bridle. Still, are you aware of how you would manage a horse without a lead line or bridle? If you have ever changed a horse's pasture, you have probably wondered why.

Natural horse training is a method by which you can learn to master your mind. No matter what circumstance you find yourself in with your horse, you won't have to worry about losing control if you can master their thoughts. Natural training is a particular discipline that needs to be followed correctly in order to achieve success.

It is important to realize that using the term "diěciple" for natural horse training does not imply obedience or punishment but rather that you are focusing on the horse's quiet acquiescence. To own a horse that is a good follower, you require a trainer with good self-control and discipline. In this manner, the horse will be able to follow your lead voluntarily.

In order to have this kind of successful natural horse training, trainers must concentrate on developing a patient and providing a comfortable and safe atmosphere for the horses. Although this diagram makes natural training appear simple, mastering this horse training technique is extremely challenging.

To begin this horse training method, get your horse to pay attention to you. In order to accomplish this, you must also give your horses your whole attention and what they do, avoiding allowing distractions to get in the way.

Ensure that you position yourself in a location that allows you to concentrate and focus. Should it not be feasible to carry out this task for extended periods, you ought to begin with little bursts of no more than ten minutes and gradually extend the duration.

Focusing on your horse and the feedback they provide is important. What signs are the eyes and ears giving you? What does their breathing indicate to you? What is the response rate of the horse, and how does it compare to previous times? This will assist you in identifying what prompts your horse to pay attention to you, enabling you to get their attention and accomplish your goals voluntarily.

Both relaxation and rhythm are essential for natural hair training. When you approach the hourglass, you must ensure that your actions are rhythmic. You should move comfortably even as you get closer to the stall. Additionally, you ought to pay close attention to how you breathe. Your watcher will be closely monitoring your behaviour, and they will be able to tell whether you're nervous. For this reason, relaxation and rhythm are essential in the event that anything unexpected or unforeseen occurs later.

Using these two easy steps can help you start seeing success with natural horse training. Even so, you shouldn't lose hope if things don't work out on the first day or week of training. Sometimes, it takes several months before students are able to learn how to use a non-prescriptive learning system. Even though the name of this practice is "natural horse training," not all trainers and horses will naturally engage in it.

8 The Magnificent Mr T

Retro fans will recall the television program "The A-Team," which followed a group of former soldiers as they travelled in a van, assisting local towns in defeating the bad guys. All of them were entertaining and colourful characters, but none stood out more than Mr T with his gold chains, mohawk, and motto, "I feel sorry for the fool." Fans looked forward to exciting new adventures each week from the show.

By luck, I was able to work and train under a different Mr T. A family friend of ours with multiple girls asked me to train a large bay gelding they had bought from a nearby racetrack trainer. He was about seven years old when I obtained him, well-formed at sixteen hands with an excellent pedigree. That seemed like the ideal age to begin training for barrel racing. He had a huge personality to go along with his talent, much like the Mr. T on TV!

I began working for Mr. T. while I was a first-year college student. I had plenty of time to work with him because I needed a horse, as usual, to ride and compete on. Because he was so intelligent and agile, he was relatively easy to train. Still, he was also the type of horse that required multiple trips to the races in order to truly establish himself and become competitive. For a spell, I got to carry him once a week since there was a barrel racing series going on in a town an hour away. After visiting the galleries, we headed to the racing. I was thrilled with his performance in the first race. After finishing second in the second race, my attention started to grow. Though we weren't actually moving much quicker, we were winning the series. Although it was a fantastic achievement, he was only approximately seven-tenths of a second off the winning times, and I always aim for perfection. He could have been faster, in my opinion, but he needed more competitive runs to improve.

We attended the series once a week for four weeks. He put in his best effort and placed each week, but he did not get much faster. But he was incredibly reliable. He was easy to manage, quiet in the alleyway, and never offered to shoulder into the barrels on his turns. He saw everything without missing a trick or a jump. He was easy to handle and hauled in the trailer gently. A lot of folks at the races didn't know me because I was four hours north of my hometown, attending college. They were intrigued that I was training this horse for someone else, and they asked questions. The fact that he was performing so well really impressed them. On the other hand, I was growing impatient that we weren't moving more quickly.

I trained and hauled Mr. T for two months until he was well-seasoned and prepared to compete regularly. Before he headed home, it was time for one last run. My dad arrived at the college rodeo with our family friend, Mr. T's owner, to watch and collect him after I entered him. Our run was enjoyable. Though not quick enough to finish first, it was a solid run that took roughly the same amount of time off as all the other races. Though our friend was quite happy, I was sad that I had not been able to convince him to run faster. Mr T was there for his daughter, who is in high school, and he was pleased with how easy and consistent the gelding was to manage.

After a few years, a family friend informed me about Mr. T. He wanted to sell him because his daughter was no longer riding. I consented to ride him until he made a sale. Taking a horse that

I knew how to ride was not difficult, and I would get to run him once more.

Finding a family in search of a horse for their daughter, who is in high school, didn't take long. Their family was so charming. We discussed his training and methods of operation, and the daughter found him to be simple to get along with. They soon started finishing first and second in races. They were devoted to him, and although I was sorry to see him go so fast, I was confident he would find a loving home.

I was accurate. It was a fantastic home for him. After growing up and attending college, the daughter got in touch with me to let me know that Mr. T was still a part of their family. I will always remember the large bay gelding with the humorous name, and I am overjoyed that his family felt the same way about him as I did. Most trainers never get to see the kind of long-term effects their training would have on a horse and its rider, but this time, I was fortunate enough to find out.

9 Best Outcome

My family had a difficult time growing up in the 1990s. The oil boom crashed when I was a college student. Many people were having difficult times since the economy was collapsing. With what you had, you had to make due. At that point, my dad inexplicably acquired a small brown mare of cutting breed. She hadn't learned to ride a bike until she was around four years old. One summer, he promptly put me to work breaking her.

The small mare appeared to be rather charming, but appearances may be misleading. We dubbed her Star because she was short and stocky, and she had the cutest little head ever, with a white star emblazoned on her forehead. She was as vicious as they come, I learned, when I eventually climbed on her back. Star would forcefully push herself against the fence and scrape my leg down the side of the round pen. When I would pin her, she would just stand there as I would beat her till I was free. She put on a good show on the ground, but below, she was incredibly stubborn. She gave off the impression of being a lovely little princess who would never hurt anyone.

I eventually got Star broke and rode fairly decently after the torturous summer. She didn't have much "go," so you had to give her a lot of leg kicks in order for her to lope, but she was still riding.

I was shocked when my father chose to send her to me to tie goats at the college rodeos the next spring. I had not really thought about it until now. All I wanted was something to ride, and I didn't mind teaching her how to tie goat ties. She had only ridden around for much of her life, so I knew I had a lot of training ahead of me. Tieing a goat is not that difficult. Run to the goat at the end of the arena, slow down so I can get off, and move aside. It sounds easy enough, but it's not when you have a five-year-old who is green-broke.

She had to undergo months of labour and planning to be ready. The fact that Star had never even been pulled to a rodeo let alone competed in anything, had escaped my attention. We were in the slack, which was my only hope of survival. Thus, there wouldn't be a sizable gathering or boisterous music. Perhaps the abundance of new sights to see wouldn't divert her attention. I wasn't bothered by the large coliseum used for the Snyder College Rodeo, but Star was clearly bothered by it. She bucked all the way down the arena to the goat because she was so angry. I gave it my best while riding her! I didn't stop kicking or attempting to reach the goat as quickly as possible. She found it easy to stop when we arrived because that was essentially what she wanted to do anyhow. I managed to complete the task in twelve seconds, even after jumping off and tying the goat. To put it in perspective, a time of ten or eleven might make the short go, but eight or nine would win the rodeo.

Even though we missed the short go, it wasn't by much.

The team ropers who were warming up and waiting to participate gave me some amazing scores on my ride. The announcer complimented me as well. I tried my hardest with what I had, even if it was embarrassing.

I called my father when I came home from the rodeo to tell him that this mare was simply not suitable for a goat-tying horse. He concurred.

A few months later, I hauled Star home since I didn't think she would make a decent barrel horse. My dad quickly sold her to a local man so that his daughter could attempt training on poles and barrels in preparation for 4-H competitions. After everything I had gone through with Star, I wasn't really convinced that was a smart idea, but I was mistaken. While working cows, the man rode the horse and managed to stop her from bucking. His daughter expertly trained Star, and I even got to see them perform admirably in a competition at one of their presentations. The little mare had gone a long way, and I was relieved that they intended to keep her permanently and even use her as a broodmare.

I realize now that when it comes to competition, I take myself a bit too seriously. Even when I win, I always strive to improve, so when I don't have a good run, I get down for a bit. Good is never enough, in my opinion. I am a hard-headed person who is still searching for a particular horse to run barrels on despite years of little to no luck. I would have never stopped citing that as proof that you should never give up riding if I had taken the quick go on a horse that barreled through the arena!

The paddock and stall for horses

If possible, keep your Friesian horse in a horse stall that has access to a paddock. In technical terms, it should really be named a horse shelter rather than a horse stall. To keep the horse in for at least the night, a stall should measure at least 12 by 12 feet and be closed on all four walls with a closed door. Three of the four sides of a horse shelter are closed, leaving the horse free to enter and exit at will.

There might be an access door on the shelter where you can feed your Friesian horse twice a day and bring it in or out. My shelters feature a half-door that splits, allowing us to leave the top open so your Friesian horse may frequently glance out like a window. Feeding access is also provided from the top opening. When bad weather is predicted for the night, we shut the top door.

The grain feeder is fixed to the inside of the shelter's bottom entrance, and I can access the hay rack to the right of the door. In this manner, I can add a few hay flakes to the rack and fill his feeder with a tiny pail of grain without having to open the bottom door. To lessen the amount of hay he spills on the ground, one horse requires a hay bag. For convenient feeding, the front glass also provides access to the bag.

The shelters are 12 by 12 feet. The paddocks ought to measure a minimum of 25 by 50 feet or more. You might need to do some research to find your Friesian horse the ideal living situation if you don't own a horse property and are boarding him at a facility or tiny stables. If your objective is to have a show horse, we do not advise having a stall with a daily turnout.

We advise having a pasture shelter for your Friesian horse if you choose to keep him as a full-time pasture horse. If your Friesian horse is kept on your land, you will need to remove the manure from the paddocks regularly. You can want to employ someone to fix small things around your property and tidy the paddocks. It is recommended that you clean the paddocks yourself either every day or every other day. The more often you perform it, the less labour it is and the fewer insects and parasites your Friesian horse will have to deal with.

After seven days in the cold, I cleaned paddocks. Every paddock held an ample amount of manure. You have a lot of work ahead of you if the weather prevents you from cleaning. Because of this, we advise daily cleaning whenever it is practical. Until the manure transforms into fertilizer, it should be kept in a manure bin. You have two options: either scatter the fertilizer over your pastures or charge $10 per truckload for it. Gardens can also take advantage of it. You can either purchase or hire a tractor with a front-end loader and mower if you own a horse stable. When the weeds start to grow, you can use the tractor to mow your pastures at least twice a year. Once a month, you can mix your manure mound with the front-end loader.

Twice a year, you can spread fertilizer using a front-end loader. A harrow might also be used to aid in spreading the manure over the pasture. Here are a few benefits of boarding your Friesian horse at a local stable. You just pay your board dues each month. The owner of the stable is in charge of all general farm care, including purchasing a tractor and implements, cleaning manure, and providing feed.

Additionally, the contract states that the owner shall provide you prompt notice if any health issues emerge. In case of an emergency, you should also provide the stable owner with your veterinarian's phone number. It's actually a pretty decent deal if you only have one Friesian horse, and the going rate in your area is between $400 and $500. Plus, you get to spend more time with your new best buddy face-to-face!

Why a pasture and stall for horses are ideal

For the most part, a paddock and horse stall are ideal for your Friesian horse. Your Friesian horse can be indoors or outdoors at will if it has a horse stall and pasture. Despite spending the night locked in the paddock every night, he feels more liberated. When you take your Friesian horse inside and when you let him out, you will be the only one in charge. The grass will grow at its fastest in the late spring and early summer.

As was previously indicated, an excessive amount of sugar in the grass might cause a Friesian horse to founder. Your Friesian horse may succumb to laminitis as a result of the founder. An afflicted horse will frequently be put to death, which is an extremely traumatic event.

We only let our horses go outside for two to three hours a day during the season of rapid growth. We receive a lot of rain in the autumn, winter, and spring. The pasture is unsuitable for horses, and the rain creates pools. We only let them graze for one or two hours each day, and on certain days, we don't let them out at all.

On most other days, if the weather permits, we might let them outside for up to ten hours a day. I attempt to let them outside whenever I can because they graze for exercise for the entire time and consume roughly one pound of grass every hour. I just need to feed the horses 10–20 pounds of hay per night if they are out for 10 hours. Thus, all parties benefit. It's conceivable that

Friesian horses eat more quickly in order to eat enough feed.

Fresh pasture grass consistently yields superior results than hay, and your Friesian horse will always favour grazing and exercise. When grazing all day, your Friesian horse will cover about 8 miles in a single day. Additionally, your hay expenses are reduced. Every year, your Friesian horse can consume up to 10,950 pounds of grass or hay. One horse would require about 100 bales of hay if you purchase the 3-string bales at a cost of 110 pounds apiece and feed him solely hay without any pasture grass. Each year, you can get a whole semi-trailer load of hay for a reasonable price per bale. Alternatively, you can purchase 10–20 bales at a time individually.

Here in my area, we spend close to $23.00 per bale for 3-string orchard grass. At that price, each horse's monthly hay costs range from over $100.00 to $200.00. Each horse needs 30-45 pounds of vitamins every month. At $23.00 a bag, a 50-pound bag of vitamins can last a horse for 25 to 50 days. At $12.00 for fifty pounds, COB (corn, oats, and barley) is significantly less expensive. A horse can go nearly a month on one bag of COB.

Horse treats come in 20-pound sacks, costing $12.00 each, and one bag will sustain a horse for almost three months. As you can see, when your horse spends less time in the pasture, the costs increase. Here are some additional benefits of boarding your equine. You and your Friesian horse would, however, both prefer boarding or owning a horse property with a paddock that has shelter and daily grazing time.

Your Friesian horse will need a few days to adjust to the stall.

Your new home will seem unusual to your Friesian horse at first because most of them are content when they have a pasture buddy. Your Friesian Horse will have a partner to share the pasture with at turnout time if there is another horse in the adjacent paddock. The stalls are frequently connected yet distinct. Since they can frequently hear each other breathe, snort, or whine in the attached stall, neither horse will feel lonely during the night.

When your Friesian horse has been in his paddock and accustomed to his pasture companion for two or three days, it's a good idea to start developing a bond with him. Just put on his halter and give him a good brushing on the first day. After giving him a brief tour, put him back in his paddock. You can do the same on the second day, but this time, saddle him up, put on his harness, and take him for a short stroll. Increase your activities with him little by little each day that you work with him. After a week or so of warm-up exercises, do not attempt to ride him.

Choosing the Ideal Home for Your Friesian Horse

Although we have discussed a lot of this already, your Friesian horse must live in the ideal house and surroundings. We've talked about the benefits of having your Friesian horse in a paddock with a shelter and a pasture buddy to keep him company when he spends nearly all of his time in the pasture.

You will have far greater influence over the welfare of your Friesian horse if you own the farm. It's not quite perfect, but you might have to choose the best area if you're boarding your Friesian horse. There might not be a lot of options available to you. There might only be two or three stables in the neighbourhood. For a variety of reasons, you might take your Friesian horse to one place and then relocate him to your second choice a month later. You need to think about the needs for care, nutrition, a pasture buddy, communication with the stable owner, and shelter.

You may need to move your "Alpha" gelding Friesian horse to a new pasture if he is fighting with another Alpha horse in the pasture. You must get along well with the stable owner if you are boarded. Don't be afraid to recommend that he select a different horse that your Friesian horse will get along with. You won't have to relocate your Friesian horse if a better pasture buddy can be found. For a young horse, making too many moves too quickly can be traumatizing.

Where to Get a Friesian Horse at

The only choice available to you if you don't own a horse property is to board your Friesian horse. Owners of Friesian horses frequently choose to purchase a second and even a third animal. Financial issues become important very early if you are boarding. You might start thinking about buying a small stable for you and your horses to live in instead of boarding if your monthly rent or house payment is $1200.00 and your monthly boarding expenses are between $1000.00 and

$1500.00. If your study indicates that a 3-bedroom house and a 5-acre horse ranch would cost about $1900.00 for a mortgage, you might decide that this is less expensive than boarding.

Even some maintenance expenses and food would be covered by your ample funds. Please remember to account for the entire amount of time needed for maintenance. General ranch care will take up a significant amount of your time if you work 40 hours a week and can only spend 20 hours with your Friesian horse. Often, the extra time will take up time that you could have spent with your horses.

Ways To Improve Your Classes On Horse Riding

But not every activity allows people to form bonds with animals. Riding horses is the best outdoor sport you can undertake. People can spend quality time with horses and bond with them through this outdoor pastime. Horseback riding lessons allow people to enjoy themselves while learning how to care for the animal.

You must abide by the regulations if you want to enjoy the many advantages of participating in this outdoor sport. People should ride horses correctly by following a few easy rules. It is advised that novices approach the horse with assurance. Confidently approaching a horse will affect how it feels about you.

People need to realize that horses do not purposely hurt people. You will only be harmed by these animals if you are anxious. Horses can detect when their riders are anxious, and this influences how they behave. For the animal to have a nice ride, people must, therefore, have a good attitude.

In order to protect themselves throughout the activity, aspiring riders should exercise caution when riding horses. The animal must be mounted as the next phase in the training process. You may assist your horse and yourself in developing trust by correctly mounting the animal. You should follow a few guidelines to make sure you can sit securely on the animal.

Holding the stirrups under your arm, make sure the length is appropriate. Place your arm on the saddle and measure the stirrup with your arm to make sure the length is appropriate. Remember that the length of the stirrup should match the length of your arm.

It is recommended that novices utilize extra assistance to mount correctly. To mount the horse, you need to utilize both hands and legs. If you want to maximize your chances of a successful mount, position yourself to the left of the animal. You should be able to hold the horse's reins and mane with your left hand. As you place your left foot in the stirrup, your right hand should assist you in turning the stirrups. To help you hold the saddle, use your right hand. With your right foot, raise yourself while holding onto the saddle with your right hand. You can more easily mount the horse by using your right foot to assist in placing weight on your left foot. To improve your chances of riding comfortably, make sure your weight is distributed evenly across your back. Because holding the reins hard will cause the horse to stop, riders should hold the reins loosely to prevent confusion.

You can ride a horse without difficulty if you take riding lessons. It is advised that people ride horses calmly in order to prevent falls from the back. It is recommended that people enrol in expert horse care lessons. Using trained horses is a great way to pick up riding skills.

Horses can be trained to walk by using a certain sound and motion. If you gently kick the horse while squeezing your legs against its body and clucking loudly, the horse will be able to walk. Horseback riding might be challenging, but there are some basic rules that people can follow. To tell the horse to turn left or right, you should use your legs. To turn the animal in the desired direction, hold the reins with both hands.

You should draw the reins toward you while yelling "whoa" to stop these creatures. You should dress comfortably when riding to guarantee your safety. Steer clear of clothing that flutters. Lost clothing typically flaps, frightening the animal and leading to mishaps. Wearing anything that could catch on an animal's body is not advised. Enrolling in horseback riding instruction has numerous benefits.

Learning to ride a horse gives people more self-assurance when interacting with animals. You know how to take care of your horse and can communicate with it. Students pick up appropriate behaviour skills. This is a result of education regarding animal health care.

Riding classes are enjoyable because they facilitate student connection. Participants in these classes strengthen their muscles and strengthen their minds.

The majority of horses require hoof trims every six to eight weeks. You may either hire a farrier to come and trim for you, or you can learn how to do this with a trimmer and file. The trimmer resembles a hybrid of a nail clipper and a set of enormous pliers. The rough file is really huge. Most of the time, the hoof can be filed smoothly in a few strokes after reducing it to a ¼ to ½ inch. Avoid cutting the hoof too short, as this may cause bleeding. After clipping, some horse owners choose to always shoe their mount.

Some horses can walk anywhere without shoes because of their extremely strong hooves. Some people find it difficult to walk on jagged pebbles or stones. Strap-on shoes are an additional choice. These can be taken off when not needed and put on when needed. You may choose to wear shoes exclusively on your front two feet. Since a horse would often place most of his weight on his front foot, this is usually sufficient.

At the very least, you should have a farrier trim your horse when you initially get it done. Should you want to trim yourself in the future, please take great care with the trimming. Costly are farriers. "You need to start with a large fortune if you want to have a small fortune after owning horses for a few years," it is said. Another proverb goes, "The human brain is the most amazing organ in the human body; it thinks and functions well every day, 365 days a year, from the moment of your birth, until you fall in love with a horse." Thus, you might use this as a caution about the total cost of owning your horse in the long run.

As you read this book, we anticipate that it will already be too late for you. Either you and your horse are already in love, or you are in love with the thought of getting your first horse. In any case, it's probably too late to heed any caution. As I've already indicated, horses can be dangerous. It is estimated that 100 people die in the US each year from riding or handling horses; most of these deaths are accidental, and the horse did not want to kill the victim. An estimated 1000–2000 head injuries occur annually, most of which are treated with survival but leave the victim permanently altered. Again, for this reason, we advise you to use a safety helmet when riding.

The Teeth of Your Horse

Horses have teeth designed for grazing.

There are 12 incisors in the front of the mouth of an adult horse.

The premolars and molars are two of the 24 teeth that are designed for chewing.

"Tushes" are the extra four canine teeth that stallions and geldings have located just beneath their incisors.

In front of the molars, some horses—male and female alike—will also acquire one to four tiny vestigial teeth, or "wolf," teeth.

A horse's teeth can be used to determine how old it is.

Throughout life, teeth erupt and become worn down from grazing.

Horses experience variations in the angle at which the chewing surfaces touch, as well as a characteristic wear pattern and tooth form.

Horses' ability to digest food is hampered if their teeth lack a flat surface on which to chew.

Regular dental examinations are a good idea, but no more than once a year is recommended.

Typically, veterinarians advise having your horse's teeth floated every one to four years, but preferably by the time the horse is ten years old.

The act of filing down all of the sharp points and edges to create a level chewing surface is known as "floating" your horse's teeth.

Increased revenue and outlays for your budget!

Eyes: Of all land mammals, horses have the largest eyes.

Horses can see over 350 degrees, and they have great day and night vision.

Similar to red-green colour blindness in humans, horses have partial colour blindness.

Your veterinarian should examine your horse's eyes on a regular basis. Every day, you ought to examine your horse's eyes. Regular inspection of his stall and paddock is necessary to remove any sharp or pointed objects, such as loose nails or screw tips poking through.

Additionally, search for and remove any loose, sharp wires or splinters. The reason is that one of your horse's eyes could get punctured. During one of your routine inspections, you might discover that your horse's eye is almost completely swollen shut. It's likely that some grit, dust, or grass fragment merely scratched your horse's eye. Try using a medicine called "Vetericyn" Ophthalmic Gel for irritated eyes before calling the veterinarian. After cleaning your hands, apply a thick layer of gel to your fingertip and place it slightly above his lower eyelid. He'll undoubtedly want to move away from you but resist the urge to let him touch your hand with his eye. His eye is itching, and it feels wonderful, so he'll want to do that. This will assist in distributing the gel across his eyeball's surface.

Remove All Potential Injury Risks

Horses are incredibly muscular creatures. Its entire body is composed of a group of muscles that are joined to its skeleton. Their musculoskeletal system serves as an intermediary between their backbone and their front legs. In order to prevent a shortage of circulation, their feet pump blood in and out like second hearts. Horses that exercise regularly remain healthy and injury-free all the time. This is particularly true for horses who aren't utilized in physically taxing tasks all the time; if a horse is left in the stable without regular exercise, poor blood circulation may cause swollen feet. Light, regular training routines can easily prevent this.

Heart arrhythmia

Arrhythmia has been reported in horses on occasion. An arrhythmia occurs when a horse's heart skips beats, causing irregular heartbeat. In such situations, heart rate monitors are typically rendered ineffective because they are unable to generate heart rate readings. It is crucial to physically take the horse's pulse or heart rate using a stethoscope. This will enable you to determine whether or not the horse's heart rate is regular.

Lack of water

The level of hydration in a horse directly affects the amount of blood in its body. The heart of a horse is supposed to circulate blood throughout the body once every minute. The number of heartbeats per minute required for blood to flow through every portion of the horse is known as the heart rate. When the blood volume is lower than usual, the horse will need to pump blood through all of its organs and body parts more often than it would in a typical volume situation. This causes the heart rate to rise above average even in the absence of any physical activity.

Diverse Excitement Levels

The degree of eagerness varies across horses. A horse's heart rate increases above average when it becomes excited. As a result, the horse's heart rate will be higher than it would be under normal conditions. This means that depending on the level of exercise and training being done, the heart rate shown by the heart rate monitor may be higher than what would be expected. This is something that an experienced trainer can see in the horse, and they will typically only rely on the heart rate monitor readings after the horse has calmed down and the degree of exercise is quite high.

The temperature

Horse heart rate is greatly influenced by temperature. The horse's heart rate increases with temperature. When exercising, the horse will exert more energy than when exercising in a cooler climate.

It is crucial to remember in each of the situations above that experienced horse trainers may be able to identify any irregularities in the heart rate readings and take the appropriate safety measures to prevent any harm.

A Variety Of Appropriate Balancing And Fundamental Suppling Exercises

Take some time to mentally go over the aids needed for each exercise and consider the benefits the exercise will provide for the horse before introducing and practising them. Every workout ought to have a specific goal, and it shouldn't be done carelessly for fun.

Start all exercises in walking first. You won't be able to perform the exercises in trot if you can't perform them in the walk, and you won't be able to perform them in the canter if you don't have what you are working on in the walk.

A key component of your young horse's early training is basic arena schooling figures such as walking and trotting on 20-meter circles, the outside track, or over the diagonals with changes of rein. The level of effort and accuracy required for these workouts directly relates to the benefits you receive. In particular, a 20-meter circle requires just the correct amount of bending to begin the gymnastic training that will build and supple the horse's body without unduly straining its muscles, joints, or tendons.

Start by shifting a little more weight onto your inside seatbones when riding turns, circles, etc. The horse is led into the turn and asked to flexion to the inside with the inside rein. The horse is asked to bend and is kept moving forward by the inside leg at the perimeter. To enable the horse to bend without losing the touch required to support him and keep him from going out through his outer shoulder, the outside rein must give slightly. In order to maintain the circle's shape, the outside leg helps the outside rein. To keep the rider's shoulders parallel to the horse's, the outside shoulder is slightly pulled forward. Turns and corners on a young horse should be ridden as 8 to 10 m quarter circles, not less. To develop the two sides of your horse's body, make sure you practice both reins equally.

Even well-trained horses use circles on a daily basis because they are the most effective educational figure for young horses.

You order your horse to leave the track at the first quarter marker and begin riding a loop to a specific spot (5 to 10 m off the track parallel with the halfway marker) before returning to the track when you ride shallow loops down the long side of the arena. When you leave the track, maintain the turn. When you return to the track, make a new bend before returning to the prior one until you are level with the halfway point (B or E). Begin with a 5-meter loop and work your way deeper until you reach the centre line (10-meter loop).

It is best to ride away from the outside track since many horses utilise the fence or arena wall as a prop, which hinders their ability to learn balance. Exercises involving riding away from the track (second track, quarter lines, centre line and diagonals) can help with this issue. Ride across the long diagonal, for instance, at a trot, aiming to strike the outside track approximately. To ride the approximate short side, stop 2 metres before the quarter marker. One to two metres distant from the outer track. Before turning to travel back across the diagonal and repeat the process on the opposite short side of the arena, ride straight along the short side.

Introduce and practise serpentine exercises with three loops. When performing exercises like serpentines, figures-of-eight, or similar ones, your horse must frequently switch from one hind leg to the other for weight bearing. When your horse circles, turns, or corners, the inside hind leg bears greater weight than the outside because the inside leg must follow a smaller path, and the inside hind joints must bend more than the outside ones. Regularly altering the bend in serpentine exercises will urge him to step farther under his body, improve his balance, and force him to engage his hind legs alternatively on both reins. First, move ahead at a steady trot on the "normal" serpentines. At the top of each loop, touch the outside track. Next, switch up the exercise and practise 'old-fashioned' serpentines by bending the loop over the centre line to make it resemble a bulb. You're always going around the corner.

Ride numerous walks-to-trots and walks-to-trots, as well as a large circle between walks and canters (a return to walks following one or three circles in the centre). A horse can only benefit from transitions if they are ridden correctly. Make sure you have developed a forward-moving, distinct rhythm in your walk before requesting a transition. Consistent, flexible rein contact that is supporting rather than constrictive or harsh is ideal.

Begin by teaching and practising the turn-around-the-forehand technique (see the chapter "Lateral Movements" for more details). Exercises like the turn-around-the-forehand help to relax. It develops the responsiveness to weight aids and specific rein aids and helps a young horse comprehend one-sided, lateral driving and supporting aids. This action helps the rider develop feel and coordination because most issues arise when the rider gives too strong of an aid, which causes the horse to stride too much forward or backward and become stiff and unhappy. With one hind leg stepping in front of and slightly across the other, the horse's forelegs should be taken up and put down on a very narrow arc, while his hind legs should describe an arc around the forelegs. Start by moving very slowly—one step at a time. The horse should not just turn around, maybe on all four legs.

Rotate the forehand

Simpler leg-yielding exercises (from the quarter line to the outside track and along the outside track with the horse's head to the wall/fence) should be introduced and practised. Horses typically move sideways away from alarming objects, but they still stare towards them and away from the direction of movement. This is why leg-yielding is a natural movement for horses. As soon as the young horse is able to travel freely in large circles and straight lines, the movement can be introduced. Before moving on to the working trot, perfect your walk gait. When a cyclist uses too strong of an aid, problems may arise. You will probably be more successful if you do as little as possible to communicate with your horse. See the chapter "Lateral Movements" for additional details on leg yielding.

Leg-yielding with the horse's head towards the wall or fence and from the quarter line to the outside track

Practise extending the horse's front and rear at the trot.

Some Gipsy Vanner horses can walk anywhere without shoes because of their exceptionally strong hooves. Some people find it difficult to walk on jagged pebbles or stones. Strap-on shoes are an additional choice. These can be taken off when not needed and put on when needed. You may choose to wear shoes exclusively on your front two feet. Since a Gipsy Vanner Horse will typically place most of his weight on his front foot, this is frequently sufficient.

At the very least, you should have your Gipsy Vanner Horse trimmed by a farrier the first time. Should you want to trim yourself in the future, please take great care with the trimming. Costly are farriers. You may take this as a warning about the costs you will incur over the lifetime of your Gipsy Vanner Horse. Some sayings go, "If you want to have a small fortune after owning horses for a few years, you need to start with a large fortune," and "The human brain is the most amazing organ in the human body; it thinks and works well constantly from before you are born 24/7 and 365 days per year, until you fall in love with a horse."

As you read this book, we anticipate that it will already be too late for you. Either you already adore your Gipsy Vanner horse, or you adore the thought of owning a Gipsy Vanner horse for the first time. In any case, it's probably too late to heed any caution. I have also emphasised the potential danger associated with Gipsy Vanner Horses. It is estimated that 100 people die in the

US each year from riding or handling a Gipsy Vanner horse; most of these deaths are accidental, and the horse did not intend to murder the victim. An estimated 1000–2000 head injuries occur annually, most of which are treated with survival but leave the victim permanently altered. Again, for this reason, we advise you to use a safety helmet when riding.

The Teeth of Your Horse

Horses have teeth designed for grazing.

There are 12 incisors in the front of the mouth of an adult horse.

The premolars and molars are two of the 24 teeth that are designed for chewing.

"Tushes" are the extra four canine teeth that stallions and geldings have located just beneath their incisors.

In front of the molars, some horses—male and female alike—will also acquire one to four tiny vestigial teeth, or "wolf," teeth.

A horse's teeth can be used to determine how old it is.

Throughout life, teeth erupt and become worn down from grazing.

Horses experience variations in the angle at which the chewing surfaces touch, as well as a characteristic wear pattern and tooth form.

Horses' ability to digest food is hampered if their teeth lack a flat surface on which to chew.

Regular dental examinations are a good idea, but no more than once a year is recommended.

Typically, veterinarians advise having your horse's teeth floated every one to four years, but preferably by the time the horse is ten years old.

The act of filing down all of the sharp points and edges to create a level chewing surface is known as "floating" your horse's teeth.

Increased revenue and outlays for your budget!

Views

The largest eyes of any land mammal are seen in horses.

Horses can see over 350 degrees in all directions.

Horses see quite well both during the day and at night.

Similar to red-green colour blindness in humans, horses have partial colour blindness.

Your veterinarian should examine your Gipsy Vanner horse's eyes on a regular basis. Every day, you should examine the eyes of your Gipsy Vanner horse. Regular inspection of his stall and paddock is necessary to remove any sharp or pointed objects, such as loose nails or screw tips poking through.

Additionally, search for and remove any loose, sharp wires or splinters. The reason is that he could pierce one of your Gipsy Vanner Horse's eyes. You might discover that your Gipsy Vanner Horse's eye is almost completely swelled shut during one of your daily inspections.

It's likely that your Gipsy Vanner Horse just has a small piece of grass, dust, or grit in his eye. Try using a medicine called "Vetericyn" Ophthalmic Gel for irritated eyes before calling the veterinarian. After cleaning your hands, apply a thick layer of gel to your fingertip and place it slightly above his lower eyelid. He'll undoubtedly want to move away from you but resist the urge to let him touch your hand with his eye. His eye is itching, and it feels wonderful, so he'll want to do that. This will assist in distributing the gel across his eyeball's surface.

Should the oedema not subside within a day, you can choose to schedule a stable appointment with your veterinarian. Even after losing one eye to blindness, some horses can still be ridden and function normally most of the time. Some horses go totally blind, but if there's no possibility of a stumble, they could be able to be ridden in mild terrain. That would only happen in a lifetime partnership between a really strong horse and rider. This book is actually meant to educate you on how to create, tend to, and grow that same kind of lifetime relationship.

The lifespan of a horse is 25 to 30 years. Some Horses survive into their forties and sometimes even older. In the 1800s, there was a horse that was reported to have lived for 62 years. A 56-year-old pony is said to have passed away in 2007.

The friendship and affection you share with your Gipsy Vanner Horse will only deepen with each passing year, even if the majority of it will blossom in the first year. I used to enjoy giving my horse a hug around the base of his neck, pressing my face up against it to smell him, and pressing my chest up against him. I used to do this with him before I bought him to make sure he was a docile horse with whom I could develop a bond.

To avoid undesirable tendencies in your Thoroughbred horse early on:

Don't be scared to reprimand them.

Tell him "No" forcefully if he nips your arm.

When he fidgets when being touched at the hitching rail, tell him "No."

Early instruction on what is acceptable and unacceptable can help him become a more obedient horse and reduce the need for corrective action in the future.

He will learn that you are in charge and that he must pay attention to you if you stop any negative behaviour and start a positive one in its place. He really wants something from you, believe it or not. Start by telling him what actions are appropriate and what are not. Be stern but not mean.

Yelling and harsh punishment should be avoided since they might cause lifelong stress to your thoroughbred horse. You want him to respect you with a sense of pride in his heart, not to be terrified of you. When it comes to training your Thoroughbred horse, all it takes is a stern "No" and a redirection to another activity. It's now appropriate to begin your Thoroughbred horse's light training. Naturally, we go into great detail about that in this book on horse training.

Additionally, show him around his stall and paddock and explain that they are secure places for him to go for solitude and weather protection. Never use the paddock as a punishment; otherwise, you risk instilling in him a deep dislike and a lifelong avoidance of it. It won't take long for you to discover that your thoroughbred horse adores his paddock and connects it to security, hay, vitamins, grains, and clean water.

It is necessary to arrange for a farm visit from your reliable veterinarian to make sure your thoroughbred horse is healthy and has received the necessary vaccines and worming. Pay attention to any advice given regarding nutrition, exercise, training, and any health issues.

When your thoroughbred horse's hooves grow too long, keep an eye on them and make an appointment with your reliable farrier for a hoof trim. Pay attention to all advice, even if it says your thoroughbred horse would benefit from shoes or has powerful hooves. Here are some suggestions that you may decide to heed.

Viewpoint (Yours)

You must start serious training your Thoroughbred Horse as soon as he has become used to his paddock. That is to say, you can now teach him things on a long lead line or in a circular enclosure with success. We'll go into great detail about this in our next chapters. To help him become acclimated to his surroundings, make sure you stroll with him. To help him overcome his concerns and learn to accept the world as it is, expose him to a wide range of people, horses, and locations. The Thoroughbred Horse socialises during its whole life. You can't keep him in the paddock, never let him interact with people, and then expect him to act normally when he does. It takes a lifetime to socialise and teach your thoroughbred horse. Daily little steps will make a big difference.

Fear Embracing and Getting Over It

Remember that horses experience periods of fear imprinting. In these stages, phobias may emerge in your horse. Any unfavourable stimuli have the potential to permanently damage your horse, giving him a lifelong terror.

For example, if a guy mistreats your horse during this phase, he may develop a fear of all men. If a child is constantly tugging on his tail, he may develop a fear towards children.

Try to keep your horse from being scared by things that terrify him, such as loud noises like fireworks on July 4th, shouting in rage, or activities that could cause him unnecessary harm. At no point in his life should you be overly strict with him; instead, be kind. Take him on frequent walks around the stables to expose him to normal environmental stimuli, such as traffic and loud music, to help him overcome his scared attitude and learn that most stimuli are harmless. He will become less fearful the more you expose him to the outside world.

Naturally, some horses experience strange phobias. When he was left alone in the stables without any other horses to accompany him, my horse became fearful. Every day, I took him farther and farther. I would force him to go a little farther and stand for five minutes every day before I came back. I kept saying, "Good boy, good boy, good boy," to him each time. After about five minutes, we had moved out enough that he was unable to see the other horses. We carried on for an hour-long trail ride as he didn't appear to be experiencing any more concerns about it. He never again felt afraid to go out on his own. For both of us, it took an entire bag of goodies to get over that one. On the bright side, we did manage to get a good amount of exercise.

How Much Your Andalusian Horse Should Be Fed

Your Andalusian horse's endurance, age, activity level, and size all affect how much you feed him. If you can feel your Andalusian horse's ribs, you can tell if he needs to be fed more. You can tell if you are feeding him enough if his ribs are not showing through. You will need to reduce his feed if he starts to get fat on his ribs. The following is a general feeding guideline for grass or hay: 2% of the horse's daily body weight. This is predicated on the projected total quantity of nighttime hay and/or pasture grass. Recall that some Andalusian horses are considered "easy keepers," meaning that they might only require ten to fifteen pounds of hay per day. Keep an eye out; if he is dropping hay on the ground rather than eating it, you should feed him a little less hay until you discover he is consuming it all.

Keep in mind that this is only a general guideline that you can modify as necessary. However, bear in mind that an adult Andalusian horse weighs approximately 1000 pounds, so you should feed him about 20 pounds of grass or hay every day.

When to Feed Your Horse an Andalusian

For horses to consume at least 20 pounds of hay every day, they must eat continuously. I've witnessed show horses being confined to stalls for up to 23 hours every day. In the winter, I've witnessed them being kept in the stall under heat lamps and blankets. They take this action to prevent the horse from developing a winter coat. In the world of show horses, a winter coat is not fashionable. We're thinking that if you owned a show horse, you would probably buy a training guidebook tailored specifically to show horses instead of this book.

The majority of people do not board horses in pastures without the need for regular feeding. Most Andalusian horses have two daily feedings—in the morning and the evening. You will allow your Andalusian horse to graze in the pasture for the majority of the day following the morning feeding. Your Andalusian horse will learn after a few days that the evening feed consists of grain and vitamins. When you call your Andalusian horse into his paddock to give him his preferred meal, he will anticipate it.

They adore grains and vitamins. It resembles a prize or a treat. They will soon pick up on the fact that you should yell his name or give a loud, sharp whistle. When you call him in, find a safe spot to stand since he might charge you at full speed. Although there is little chance that your Andalusian horse will run you over, it is safer to stand close to a fence post or other object that you are certain he won't run into for your safety. You will eventually get enough confidence in your Andalusian horse to ensure that he never touches you or runs you down when entering their paddock.

Feeding your Andalusian horse twice a day allows for more time for interaction, training, and bonding. When you offer your Andalusian horse their favourite grain and vitamin combination, they will come to associate you with it. You will become his favourite human and will step up a notch if you feed your Andalusian horse twice a day (personally). If you are the one feeding him, this dynamic will probably happen sooner.

Being the herd's alpha leader and establishing your dominance are important aspects of horse management. For the time being, being an Alpha Status means you get to eat first; we explore this in our last chapter. Although it might appear insignificant, it plays a significant role in developing your alpha. You must wait patiently for your Andalusian horse to finish eating before he does. By doing this, you demonstrate your dominance and show your Andalusian Horse that you are in charge. Even before you call him in, he can be waiting in his paddock for feeding time. This is not going to happen every time the grass is in its active growing season. He might even have preferred the delectable fresh growth of grass to his food during that time. To begin training your Andalusian horse, you might need to go outside with him, put a halter on, and walk him to the paddock a few times. Probably the first few times, your Andalusian Horse will follow if he has a pasture companion who comes in immediately away.

Changing Foods

It can eventually become evident that, for a variety of reasons, switching to hay or grain is necessary. Use this switching schedule to swap out brands or types of food:

Day 1-2 Blend ¼ new and ¾ old meals.

Combine days 2-4 with day 1

Day 5-6: Combine ½ new and ¼ old.

Day 7: All new food, 100%

You should begin gradually, as mentioned above, while transferring your Andalusian horse from Alfalfa to Orchard Grass Hay, for example. It's a good idea to try your Andalusian horse on Orchard Grass or another grass hay if you find that he is becoming jacked up on lucerne due to its increased protein content. You'll probably notice that his behaviour has improved. You could choose to use "Mare Magic" on your Andalusian mare in order to balance her mood based on her cycles. Her behaviour will probably improve, and you will notice it. Mare Magic can likewise improve a Gelding's mood. If you see that your Andalusian horse has too much fat on his ribs, you may choose to cut back on his nutrition.

In order to help your Andalusian horse gain weight again, you can decide to add some rice bran to his diet after seeing that you can feel or see his ribs. It is customary to modify or alter your Andalusian horse's diet in order to preserve optimum health. It is advised that you get in touch with your veterinarian for further guidance if you are ever unsure.

Healthy Snacks and Treats

You can include the following nutritious human meals in your Andalusian horse's diet or give him as treats:

A delight of oats and molasses

Muesli and apple snacks

Pears and Apples

Different treats for horses from your feed store

Pumpkin or squash Carrots

Working Out With Your Andalusian Horse

The health of your Andalusian horse depends on exercise. Andalusian horses require activity to keep healthy, just like people do. As he ages, a sedentary Andalusian horse is more likely to develop obesity, heart issues, joint issues, and muscular problems. Not to mention, a bored Andalusian horse might become unruly due to a lack of activity. It's important to provide your Andalusian horse with plenty of exercise and unstructured outside activities in his pasture.

Andalusian horses need to exercise for anywhere between thirty minutes and two hours every day. Andalusian horses require two hours or more of exercise and pasture time daily. By letting him run around in his pasture, you may give him some of this exercise. You have to take the initiative for some of this work. When he has finished his feed in the morning, go into his paddock, put on his halter using the lead line, and tie him (leaving some slack) to the hitching rail.

Take out his brushes and give his entire body a thorough brushing. Remove all the tangles by brushing his mane and tail. The second and third days won't have many tangles if you brush your Andalusian horse's mane and tail every day. After cleaning your Andalusian horse, put on his blanket and saddle if you plan to ride him for the day's exercise.

It's crucial to give your Andalusian horse a thorough brushing each time before putting on the saddle. Make sure you brush out any burrs, foxtails, and dirt. Your Andalusian horse won't be thrilled if you saddle him with a burr between his skin and the saddle. We advise taking lessons before you ride your Andalusian horse if this is your first horse and you have never done so. Additionally, you can learn how to bridle and saddle your Andalusian horse. You can put on his harness after adjusting the cinch of his saddle. Fasten his reins to the saddle horn (in the case of a western saddle) or, in the case of an English saddle, around the base of his neck close to the saddle. If you have a round enclosure, attach his long lead rope and take him to the middle of an empty pasture.

In order to warm up your Andalusian horse's muscles, you can basically exercise him by having him walk, trot, or canter in circles around you. We will talk more about particular exercise training later. As a general guideline, perform ten canters, ten trots, and ten circles to walk to the left. Walk, trot, and canter to the right, then reverse course and repeat. He will be warm enough to ride after this. Additionally, it will help him release some of his stored energy, which will improve his behaviour when riding after.

You're prepared to ride now. In order to minimise lifting your leg high enough for your stirrups, you could decide to employ a mounting block. Still, you must be able to mount in both directions. Introduce him gently. First, ride him for ten to fifteen minutes. The following day, try 15-20, then 20–25, and so on, following the same pattern until you reach one hour a day. As long as you are riding in an indoor ring, nothing should go wrong. Your Andalusian horse could get afraid to leave the stable if you are heading out to ride on a trail.

"Wow!" is another way to express it. Put minimal pressure on the reins and allow your horse to move freely. You must apply gentle pressure; avoid pulling. By adding a pound or two of pressure and securing your hands without pushing or letting the reins slack, you can help the horse slip as far as possible.

The majority of horses respond well to this final method. Say "Wow!" and wait a little before applying rein pressure, releasing your hand, and allowing the reins to slack—just a little—but not excessively. The horse would come to a near-instant stop. As long as the reins are loose, the horse will keep gliding.

Allow your horse to regain control of the reins if you notice that it is starting to let go of the stop. Throughout the slide, this series of soothing motions is continued until the horse stops completely.

The complete whoa-set-slack method appears to be effective because the horse may enter the slide on its own in a matter of seconds after receiving a verbal command. His hooves sink into the ground more smoothly if he is startled by the "wow" and simultaneously maintain control over the pressure.

A quick tug on the reins tells the horse to stay in the slide as his hooves settle and begin to slide. Release the reins right away to allow the horse to slide wherever he pleases. The horse's hooves would go deep if you applied continuous pressure, which would stop the slip early. Additionally, it may make the horse rigid and pull.

A fast set slack will warn the horse to stay on the slide in case he tries to halt it. Reversing the reins should only be done if you believe the horse is beginning to emerge from the chute. Considering that lengthy swipes only take a few seconds, this setup relaxation also occurs fairly quickly. To get this right, the rider needs to be aware of the horse's feelings.

Relaxing his body is the final essential step a rider needs to take in a cue stop. As you ride, your body will provide energy to help the hose speed forward. You have to stop when you ask to stop. To be more precise, you need to sit down, ease into the saddle, stop riding, and limp your thighs, shoulders, and back.

Your horse will recognise and react to your relaxed body as a stop cue right away. The timing is crucial. If you don't provide the signal to stop riding, your horse will sense the shift in body language and stop before you mean to. This may ruin the slideshow.

For your horse to glide as smoothly as possible, how you arrange your body is crucial. It requires repetition. There won't be any long slideshows between you and your horse overnight. Just maintain your concentration and practise consistently. Sooner or later, the two of you will be together.

After The Ride: Valuable Teachings On Horsemanship

Although the term "horsemanship" is commonly used to refer to the ability to handle and ride horses, it actually refers to much more, such as knowledge of horses and an awareness of their requirements and nature. Sometimes, caring for the horse both before and after a ride is more important than actually riding to develop true horsemanship skills. Many riders never quite get the hang of being a true horseman.

This is frequently demonstrated rather plainly by the way the rider handles the horse after the ride is over.

Does he return with the horse sweaty and lathered, stopping briefly to untack the animal before hurriedly heading to his vehicle? Or does he?

After a ride, take the time to let his horse calm down, making sure that his flanks aren't heaving, that his sweat is drying, and that his nostrils aren't still flared.

If it's hot outside, hose the horse down or brush the dried sweat patches with a curry.

Put on his halter and take him outside to unwind and consume some grass while he cools down.

To make sure the horse didn't get hurt during the ride, run his hands along its legs.

Examine the horse's hooves to make sure the frog is free of stones, as this could cause discomfort and perhaps result in a stone bruise.

While the horse is still cooling off, give him a few sips of water and make sure his bucket is filled.

The majority of novice riders are unaware of the amount of planning and recovery time a horse needs both before and following a ride. This is the rider's chance to spend some valuable time bonding with the horse; do you really want the horse to think that all you do when you're riding it is work?

Thorough grooming of the horse is not only beneficial to his overall health after the ride, but it is also necessary for his welfare. During an exercise, he usually gets sweat on his back under the saddle and behind his neck, and the dried sweat is itchy. You will have to wait till the sweat has dried because brushes cannot be used to groom damp sweat. In the winter, your horse might need to wear a cooler, which is lightweight horse wear that resembles a blanket and is made of fleece, to keep him warm while his sweat dries. If not, he might become chilled if it's extremely cold.

You might start by currying the sweaty regions in circles once the sweat has dried. To push any remaining dust and grime from the coat up and off, use a stiff brush and lengthy, flicking strokes. Make careful to brush the regions where the bridle rests, both in front of and behind your horse's ears, using a face brush. Those regions might also be perspiring. Seize the chance to examine his face and confirm that his ears and eyes are clear. Make sure he doesn't have bit rubs by looking at the sides of his lips.

smooth your horse's coat once you've adequately cleaned him of any dried sweat, muck, or grime. To add a little shine, you may also use a finishing wipe. Just be careful not to spray or apply shine formulations where your horse's saddle or girth would normally sit. While the oils and silicon in them are great for enhancing the sheen of the rest of his coat, they can make the saddle and saddle pad slip during a ride.

You have now completed your ride and post-ride care. To make your horse's day complete, give him or her a few treats or let them graze on some grass.

Chapter 7: Preventing Diseases and Improving Horse Health

Although they are powerful creatures, horses are not invulnerable. They may experience one or more injuries or a variety of illnesses. There will always be sporadic episodes of illness, even with the finest of treatments.

It is your responsibility as a horse owner to lower the likelihood and severity of these conditions. Even when they do happen, you should be able to spot the warning symptoms of poor health in yourself, take prompt action to cure any wounds or illnesses, and make sure your horse gets the care it needs.

How to Tell Whether Your Horse Needs Attention

Knowing when to take care of your horse is a crucial skill for any owner. Even though a horse cannot communicate with you to let you know when it is sick, you should be able to recognise the symptoms of a sick horse and know how to properly take care of it by being aware of them and keeping a close eye out for them. The following are indications that your horse may be having problems.

- High temperature
- Abnormal heart rate and breathing (either too fast or too slow)
- Appetite loss
- Overheating of the limbs or feet
- Emission from the mouth, nose, or eyes
- Swelling in different bodily sections
- Tolerance for exercise and sensitivity
- Colic

- Wide-open mouth or an intimidating look

Asthma breathing problems

- Recurrent coughing and strange noises
- Lameness or limping
- Sores on the body
- Digestion and constipation
- Spasms in the muscles

Here are a few indicators to be aware of. Even if the presence of these symptoms does not prove that your horse is ill, they are enough of a reason to bring your horse in to see a veterinarian for a thorough examination and diagnosis.

Skin Disorders

Ringworm

Horses are not the only animals that can have ringworm—a fungal skin illness. The skin lesions that develop on it have a circular form, hence the name. The density and extent of these lesions vary, and they might develop on the neck, saddle area, neck, or girth areas of the horse. The infection may first appear as hair spikes that later fall out and leave behind unsightly sores.

Since an affected horse's near surroundings may potentially contract the disease, it may also spread indirectly.

The best way to prevent and treat ringworm in horses is to isolate the affected animal as much as you can as soon as you see symptoms. It is also advisable to discard items such as bedding materials that the diseased horse uses. Maintaining strict hygiene is essential to stopping the spread of ringworms. Consult a veterinarian for advice on treating the infection as well.

Rain-Scald

This type of skin infection arises from the skin being softer as a result of continuous skin immersion in water. Patchy hair loss on your horse's back and hindquarters is its defining characteristic. Matting of the hair and the appearance of weeping blisters and sores are possible at the injection site.

This illness is more severe in horses whose immune systems are already compromised. Horses without the natural lubricant that keeps their coat warm and dry may also experience it.

Non-breathable or leaking blankets can also result in rain scald since they expose a horse's back to continuous dampness.

How to avoid and treat rain scald: The best defence against rain scalds is to keep moisture away from your horse. Make sure your horse has access to a shelter away from the field and that the proper kind of horse blankets are used. Make sure your horse stall is dry, tidy and well-maintained.

Model - Samson pushing on the hip

In the event that he doesn't, go back to landing on his hip and pull from the side as before five or more times. Long-term time savings can be achieved by giving him the time and patience he needs to grasp the material. Try not to bind him before he is ready.

To be motivated by your example.

Your foal will follow you without strain or lead rope protection if you are consistent and on schedule. He will learn that when he follows you, he receives a prompt reward and that his bridle tension is released.

Make sure you take care of his ass first and especially avoid starting a fight! Make sure your cues are precise and provide relief when he fulfils your requests, letting him know what you require.

On the off event, if they are confused, most ponies will fight. We can start a conflict by asking too many questions too soon or by not offering assistance when he complies with our requests. He could move backwards as an alternative response.

Keep the strain on your lead line until your foal gets closer if he is pushing back on the lead. If you give in to him moving backwards and hand him the lead rope, he gets paid for going backwards.

When he takes a step forward or even stops returning and puts his head forward, release the rein and offer assistance. Follow him in reverse while holding the lead rope insult. In this manner, he progressively comes to understand that moving forward when he feels stressed out lessens and even eliminates that tension. When it is time for your foal to learn how to limit, this agreement will also be helpful.

One problem I've observed with certain ponies who have been raised in an unprepared society is that, when they come to me for help after breaking in when they are two years old, they come back when the lead is tense. This indicates to me that when the foal moved away from the pressure on the lead line, his owner released him and provided assistance!

He was, therefore, told that his major action should be to pull away and move in reverse when the lead rope is tense. As you can see, the rules have now totally altered for him, which makes it difficult to prepare for restricting, float stacking, and driving. Right now, instead of going backwards, he merely approaches people to ask for assistance. Although it can be fixed, it would be preferable and less confusing for your foal if it wasn't made in the first place.

Teaching Your Foal to Pick Up His Footwear

Rather than tying in the mood to assist foals in getting their feet gotten, I usually take the lead.

I begin by scouring the legs downward. Every time I massage, I start at the top and move a little lower, providing relief each time I reach the leg's highest point.

Run your hand back up his leg when (note that I said "when," not "if") he starts to back off, but do all in your power to keep your hand from falling off. If you do, it won't be a problem because occasionally, when he moves, your hands will slip off anyhow.

Hold him firmly with the lead line if he starts to wander so he may continue to circle you. He'll make you turn around. Assuming you must walk with him while keeping a hand on his wilt until he stops. At that moment, I successfully resumed scouring legs from the top, starting over.

We are warning him of what's to come by scrubbing from the top of his leg.

After he is perfectly still, ease the pressure in 10-second intervals every 10 centimetres (3 inches) as you descend the leg and reach past the knee to the foot. Relieve his discomfort by scraping up to the top of his leg.

To pick up his foot, place your entire palm over the front of his foot and press with your shoulder to shift his weight onto the opposing legs. At that moment, he uses his advantage to twist himself into a tucking position. You don't need to hold the foot for longer than a few seconds to start as foals. Just a little hello. Over several months, work your way up to 15 or 20 seconds.

Choosing front and middle feet for a brief period. Sunny and Lauren are models.

Make sure you take as much time as necessary because foals can be more sensitive when it comes to you touching their hind legs. Try using your calf rope again, assuming you have a sensitive soul and he's having trouble accepting your contact on his back legs.

With a firm grip on your lead rope, create a large circle that is about one metre (3.5 feet) in diameter. Place the circle nearly one hoof's diameter into the ground. Drive or give him a little shove to move him around till his foot is inside the circle. Wait for him to get reasonable on the other foot, and then pull on the open circle till it's idling about his sell's foundation.

If he's having a lot of trouble, you might have to push him up against a fence or into a corner. Keep in mind that he's only mildly perplexed or uncertain about what you're asking, so proceed with kindness, patience, and confidence.

Taking a Sensitive Soul by the rear.

Mitch and Dakota are models.

He will probably move around you and maybe engage in combat if you hold the lead line firmly. Lift his leg gently but firmly until it is roughly a foot off the ground.

Keep it there firmly till he stops opposing and slightly loosens up his leg. It should be your choice to feel him 'give' you his foot. Release the rope gently at that fleeting instant (don't just let it fall this time) and allow him to plant his foot.

After you and your foal are satisfied with this approach for both front and rear feet—that is, you no longer need to pass through the rope to retrieve the rear feet—and you have employed the method of scraping down the leg to obtain the foot, proceed to retrieve each foot by tapping its foundation. This will be beneficial.

Desensitise him to future clinical problems like wounds, shoeing, foot formation, and other concerns.

Perception of Depth:

Again, a horse must raise and lower its head to compare the object of interest with previously observed objects because of the limited range of their binocular vision, which makes depth perception difficult. Horses are extremely sensitive to anything that has been added, removed, or altered from what was there the last time they passed by. This can be explained by comparing the appearance of "new things" with items that are already stored in their memory.

Horses are frequently afraid to step into puddles, which makes sense, given their weak sense of depth. There are issues with both the reflected light and the "unknown" surface beneath the water. Risky footing makes it more difficult for a horse to escape if necessary.

The retina, or sensory screen at the back of the eye, contains a "visual streak" in the horse eye, which is the region with the best eyesight. In order to enhance the image's depth perception and detail, horses turn their heads to bring the object of interest inside the "visual streak's" range.

The horse's vision is impaired if tight ropes or reins constrain his head.

Unsurprisingly, these limitations lead to tension throughout the body.

Horse eyes seem to enlarge objects by up to 50% more than human eyes do. Although their vision is not as acute as a human's 20/20, it appears to be better than that of dogs and cats.

Instruction for Both Eyes:

The importance of teaching what we do on both sides of the horse can be understood from the way horse eyesight functions. "Right eye neglect" is what happens when a horse is handled exclusively with the left hand. Since there are no neural connections to develop to give him confidence while handling on the right side due to neglect, handling procedures will appear "strange" to him mentally on that side.

This relates to handling and training in every way. Horses are naturally left- or right-handed, just like humans. To put it another way, they have asymmetrical bodies like ourselves.

It is difficult for a horse to be straight in his body unless both sides of his body are trained gymnastically. It implies that there will always be some misalignment in a saddle. For both riders and horses, a symmetrical saddle on an asymmetrical horse is an ongoing source of discomfort.

The less agile side of the body requires at least two or three times more attention than the nimble side when learning a new activity. Consider how challenging it is to use our non-dominant hands to wash our teeth.

Visual cues in the environment:

The lights turning on in the winter morning signals to horses that their morning feed is coming soon if they live within sight of their owner's home. I provide hay in the late evenings for a portion of the year. She utilises the lantern I'm wearing as a visual cue to meet me at the shelter.

Our gestures and body language serve as visual cues during groundwork. The horse can typically see us by turning his head, even if we are long-reining (assuming he isn't wearing blinkers).

My horse's friend, a big white gelding, moved away, but she never stopped staring at a white Charolais cow in a far-off paddock, wondering if it was the same cow as her previous paddock pal.

Gipsy, my thoroughbred mare, was acutely aware of everything that lay beyond the far horizon. She looked straight at a rabbit hunter carrying a gun who was so far away I could hardly see him.

Okay, Aunt Sue replied. "Let's grab a bite to eat. You must be hungry. After that, we can rest for a while.

We can discuss the future after we've eaten and rested. Go upstairs to

Jack's room with your belongings, and I'll make us some scrambled eggs.

Josie recalled that Jack's room faced the corral on the left. She eased through the door and took a quick look around. The advertisements and pictures of horses were still in place. The majority included pictures of Jack on his large bay. He had rode it in the Sisters Rodeo Parade for many years, and some of the pictures had ribbons hanging next to him. What a lucky boy, Josie thought.

Josie emptied her box rather rapidly. She tucked her clothing into a drawer on her dresser. She arranged her comb and brush on top of the dresser and began surveying the space.

It had manly, square, modern oak furnishings that lacked frills and was well-appointed. The dresser, desk, nightstands, and double bed were all the same. The

The counterpane has a vivid Native American design from the Southwest. Upon initial observation, the room appeared to be occupied by Jack. But as Josie looked more closely, she saw that tiny personal objects had disappeared, and all of the drawers were empty.

Josie paid particular attention to the gaming console, X-Box, that was connected to the flat-screen TV in the corner.

"The eggs are prepared," Aunt Sue called. Josie realised she was starving and bolted down the stairs.

Would you like something special to eat for dinner? Aunt Sue enquired as they were eating.

Josie gave a headshake. How could she know what may be for supper when she had no idea what was in the cupboard?

The fresh fruit, toast, and eggs were all really tasty. It resembled a Sunday dinner. She fell instantly asleep after the delicious breakfast because she was so full. She was now burdened by her lack of sleep from the long night and the mountainous drive. She was itching to cuddle up and go to sleep like a cat.

Josie, though, assisted Aunt Sue in clearing the dishes before heading to her bed. It was incredibly simple because they had a dishwasher. Josie only needed to run the plates through the dishwasher after rinsing them off.

After cleaning the kitchen, Aunt Sue and Josie went to their beds. Josie's head hit the pillow, and she fell asleep.

21 3

Josie's cheeks started to well up with tears.

She could relate to the filly's anguish and bewilderment since Josie had similar emotions when she thought of her mother.

Josie pondered if there was anything she could do to cheer up the pretty painted foal. She also questioned who owned the horse.

Josie moved out of the willows and towards the filly slowly. The little horse glanced at her but stayed put.

Josie moved in closer. The filly now retreated, positioning its mother's body between Josie and itself.

Josie thought with patience. I would really like to be able to pet it without frightening it.

Josie took one very slow step forward. For every two steps Josie made forward, the filly took one step back. She was making progress.

For what seemed like hours, Josie and the filly danced slowly around the mare's body. Josie finally concluded that this was probably enough for the time being.

In Oregon, summertime days were lengthy. In mid-June, it didn't get dark until almost ten o'clock at night. After supper, she would have time to return downstairs.

When Josie returned, she would locate a treat to bring. An apple or a carrot has to be in the house. Perhaps it would solve the problem.

She would attempt to find out who owned the land and whether there were any horses in the canyon in the interim.

www.ingramcontent.com/pod-product-compliance
Lightning Source LLC
Chambersburg PA
CBHW052137110526
44591CB00012B/1754